HOW TO START A COURIER BUSINESS

The Essential Guide to Building Your Delivery Empire

Jeanelle K. Douglas

Copyright © 2024 by Jeanelle K. Douglas. All rights reserved. No part of this book, HOW TO START A COURIER BUSINESS, may be reproduced, stored in a retrieval system, or transmitted in any form or by any means, electronic, mechanical, photocopying, recording, or otherwise, without the prior written permission of the author, Jeanelle K. Douglas.

Table of Contents

Introduction 6

Understanding the Courier Industry 9

    Introduction to the courier sector. 12

    Market Overview and Potential Opportunities 15

    Analysis of key players and competitors. 18

    Trends and Future Prospects 23

Create a Business Plan 26

    The significance of a detailed business strategy. 29

    Legal and Regulatory Considerations 32

    Registering your courier business 35

    Understanding licenses and permits 38

    Compliance with transportation regulations 41

    Insurance requirements and liability protection 44

Establishing Operations 47

    Selecting the appropriate location for your business 51

    Developing operational processes and workflows 55

    Procuring necessary equipment and vehicles 58

Hiring and training staff 62

Building Partnerships and Networks 66

Establishing relationships with clients and vendors 69

Negotiating contracts and service agreements 73

Utilizing technology to streamline operations. 76

Establishing a solid network of delivery partners. 79

Marketing and Branding Strategy 83

Creating a distinctive brand identity 86

Identifying target customers and marketing channels. . 89

Implementing digital marketing methods. 92

Using standard advertising approaches 96

Managing Finance and Budgeting 100

Component of managing funds and budgeting for a courier business 103

Estimating startup costs and initial investment 107

Creating a financial plan and budget 110

Managing cash flow and expenses 114

Pricing strategies and revenue generation 117

Scaling and Growing Your Business 121

Evaluating growth opportunities and expansion strategies 125

    Introducing technology for scalability 128

    Expanding services and entering new markets. 133

    Creating a long-term, lucrative courier business 138

    Conclusion 141

    Final thoughts and inspiration for prospective courier business operators. 144

Introduction

In today's fast-paced world, the need for speedy and dependable courier services has never been greater. Courier companies play a key role in facilitating the flow of commodities and information across local and worldwide networks, from package delivery to document transport. If you've ever pondered establishing your own business, the courier sector offers a lucrative opportunity with a diverse range of prospective customers and services.

How to Start a Courier Business is a thorough guide that will assist ambitious entrepreneurs in navigating the complexities of beginning and running a successful courier business. Whether you're an experienced expert hoping to get into the business or a beginner looking to profit from the expanding demand for delivery services, this book will equip you with the information, skills, and tactics you need to make your entrepreneurial aspirations a reality.

In this book, we will look at every part of beginning and running a courier service, from knowing the market to building a strong brand presence and extending your operations. You'll learn how to create a sound company strategy, negotiate the legal and regulatory landscape, establish efficient operations, form strategic alliances, and execute successful marketing and branding initiatives.

Throughout the chapters, we'll use real-world examples, case studies, and insights from industry professionals to provide you with practical guidance and concrete solutions. Whether you're on a tight budget or have plenty of resources, we'll teach you how to get the most out of your investment and increase your chances of success in the competitive courier industry.

In addition, we'll look at the current trends and developments affecting the courier sector, including the advent of e-commerce, improvements in delivery technology, and altering customer tastes. In other to stay ahead of the curve and seizing new possibilities, you'll be well-positioned to prosper in an ever-changing business world.

Starting a courier service is not without its hurdles, but with the appropriate advice and drive, you can create a lucrative and sustainable operation that meets your clients' requirements while also contributing to the growth of your community. Whether you're motivated by a love of logistics, a desire for financial independence, or a dedication to providing outstanding service, this book will help you begin this exciting entrepreneurial adventure with confidence and purpose.

So, if you're ready to take the first step toward establishing your own courier empire, let's jump in and discover the fascinating world of courier business together.

Understanding the Courier Industry

Understanding the courier industry is like grasping the numerous routes of a bustling metropolis. It's a dynamic environment where speed, dependability, and efficiency are paramount. Starting a courier service requires a thorough grasp of the sector, much like studying a city's layout before embarking on a construction project. It lays the groundwork for success by helping entrepreneurs through the maze of obstacles and possibilities that lie ahead.

Imagine standing in the heart of a bustling metropolis, surrounded by towering buildings and bustling streets. Each building symbolizes a distinct aspect of the courier industry, ranging from regular courier services to specialized delivery solutions for e-commerce giants. Technological breakthroughs, new consumer behaviors, and global economic trends all contribute to the landscape's ongoing evolution.

As you travel through this urban jungle, you'll come across a broad range of courier ecosystem actors.

Rivals in the industry, from established logistics businesses with global fleets to agile startups using cutting-edge technology for last-mile delivery, are striving for market share.

But below the flash and beauty of the metropolitan skyline, there is a deeper knowledge of the courier industry's complexities. It's more than just getting items from point A to point B; it's also about providing experiences, establishing trust, and surpassing consumer expectations at every touchpoint.

This book will take you on a guided tour of the courier industry, examining its numerous features and unearthing hidden pearls of wisdom along the way. You'll learn about market trends, competitive dynamics, and new opportunities that will determine the course of your firm.

We'll dig into the complexities of logistics and supply chain management, assisting you in optimizing routes, streamlining processes, and reducing costs. You will learn how to use technology to increase productivity, track shipments in real time, and provide a consistent client experience from pickup to delivery.

Understanding the courier sector, however, entails not just traversing the physical infrastructure of highways and warehouses but also decoding the digital terrain of e-commerce platforms, smartphone applications, and online marketplaces. We'll teach you how to use these digital platforms to attract new clients, increase revenue, and differentiate your courier service in a congested industry. We will discuss the significance of developing strategic alliances and networks within the sector. From forming relationships with suppliers and manufacturers to partnering with other courier businesses for cross-border shipments, these connections will be critical for growing your reach and increasing your business.

Understanding the courier sector requires looking beyond the delivery vehicle and the goods on your doorstep. It is about embracing and capitalizing on the intricacies of a fast-changing ecology. And throughout the pages of this book, we will provide you with the knowledge, insights, and techniques you need to flourish in this ever-changing world.

Introduction to the courier sector.

In the broad panorama of business and trade, the courier sector serves as a critical fulcrum, ensuring the efficient and reliable transfer of products and documents from one location to another. It's a world where timeliness is essential, where every shipment tells a narrative, and where the success of enterprises and individuals is frequently dependent on the timely delivery of their consignments.

Opening the door to the Courier Industry is like stepping into a world in continual motion, where items traverse cities, countries, and continents in a choreographed dance orchestrated by a complex network of courier services. This introduction in "How to Start a Courier Business" prepares budding entrepreneurs by providing a glance into the dynamic environment they are about to join.

Courier vans speed through traffic on a crowded city street, their drivers navigating the urban maze with precision. These trucks are the industry's lifeblood, transporting shipments of all sizes and shapes, from critical paperwork to delicate artworks and medical supplies to anxiously anticipated online purchases.

The courier profession is more than just moving items; it's about dependability and confidence. Customers entrust courier firms with their costly items and sensitive documents, expecting them to deliver quickly and carefully. As a result, establishing a reputation for dependability and service quality is critical to the success of any courier firm.

But what drives this complicated network of logistics? In addition to cars and packaging, technology plays a significant role. From sophisticated monitoring systems that allow clients to see their items in real time to optimization algorithms that find the most effective delivery routes, technology is the foundation of contemporary courier operations.

The courier sector handles more than just local deliveries. In today's globalized world, international shipping is an important part of business. To ensure flawless cross-border delivery, couriers must handle customs rules, foreign tariffs, and various transit methods.

In terms of entrepreneurship, the courier sector provides a wealth of chances for anyone ready to jump in. There is plenty of space for innovation and expansion, whether it's starting a local delivery service for companies in a city or expanding into e-commerce logistics to assist the thriving online retail industry.

However, taking on this adventure requires more than simply a truck and a desire to deliver packages. "How to Start a Courier Business" looks into the complexities of entrepreneurship in this field, providing insights into market research, business planning, financial management, and customer service tactics related to the courier sector.

In essence, the introduction of the courier sector opens the door to a world in continual motion, where efficiency, dependability, and technical power combine to assure the smooth passage of products and data. It's a world full of potential for budding entrepreneurs willing to take on the adventure of starting their own courier service.

Market Overview and Potential Opportunities

Picture yourself on the outskirts of a bustling marketplace, surrounded by numerous opportunities waiting to be seized. This is the environment in which this book delves into the courier industry's market overview and potential opportunities.

The courier sector is a dynamic tapestry with a wide range of requirements and wants. From small companies looking for effective local delivery services to multinational organizations in need of smooth international logistics solutions, the market is rife with opportunity for those prepared to traverse it.

At its foundation, the courier sector flourishes in an ever-changing world of commerce and trade. With the development of e-commerce behemoths and retail digitization, the need for efficient delivery services has never been greater. Customers demand prompt delivery, real-time tracking, and exceptional service, providing an ideal environment for courier firms to thrive.

The COVID-19 epidemic has expedited the trend toward online purchasing, driving up demand for courier services. As more consumers prefer the ease of doorstep delivery, the courier industry's potential grows tremendously.

However, the market overview extends beyond only consumer demand. Understanding the complexities of supply chains, discovering specialized markets, and capitalizing on new trends are all critical for gaining a competitive advantage. Whether it's focusing on same-day delivery for local companies or providing specialized services for delicate or perishable items, the market offers several opportunities for innovation and uniqueness.

The worldwide nature of trade creates international opportunities. As organizations increase their global reach, the demand for dependable international shipping services rises in parallel. Couriers who can negotiate the complexities of international logistics, customs laws, and cross-border payments stand to benefit from a profitable sector with limitless opportunities.

The market overview and future prospects in the courier sector provide a picture of a dynamic and ever-changing world. It's a place where creativity meets necessity, and entrepreneurs may forge their own route across a sea of options. Aspiring courier business owners who dare to enter this market face a blank canvas ripe for painting with their individual ideas and entrepreneurial energy.

Analysis of key players and competitors.

In the dynamic courier sector, understanding the landscape of important companies and doing a comprehensive competition study is critical for prospective entrepreneurs looking to start their own courier services. This adventure takes you inside a world where entrenched behemoths and nimble startups compete for supremacy, each leaving their imprint on the logistics landscape.

The courier industry's key participants take many shapes, ranging from global behemoths with huge networks spanning continents to local heroes providing specialized service to specific communities. These firms have a tremendous impact on market dynamics by defining client expectations and establishing standards for service quality and reliability.

In this broad terrain, competition research becomes an essential tool for entrepreneurs starting their courier businesses.

It entails analyzing existing players' strengths, limitations, and strategies, as well as their market positioning and consumer interaction approaches, in order to identify chances for differentiation and innovation.

The industrial titans, whose names ring true across borders and whose presence looms big in the collective psyche of consumers, are at the forefront of competition analysis. These logistics titans have constructed powerful infrastructures and brand identities that demand worldwide confidence and reliability. Understanding their tactics and market positioning provides valuable information about industry developments and client preferences.

However, rivalry extends beyond the majors to include a plethora of smaller competitors and specialty suppliers that carve out their own niches in the sector. These businesses frequently specialize in certain services or target niche markets, using agility and creativity to compete with bigger competitors. Analyzing their tactics and success stories provides motivation for entrepreneurs looking to forge their own routes in the sector.

Competitive analysis delves into the customer experience, looking at customers' pain points and preferences in their interactions with existing courier providers. This client-centric strategy identifies areas for innovation and distinction, enabling entrepreneurs to personalize their services to meet unmet requirements and surpass customer expectations.

In the process of starting a courier service, major players and competition analysis act as guiding beacons, illuminating the route forward in the middle of a sea of opportunities and obstacles. Understanding the intricacies of business and learning from the triumphs and mistakes of current companies allows budding entrepreneurs to trace their own path to success, carving out their own niche in the complex tapestry of logistics.

In terms of significant actors, it is critical to appreciate the courier industry's diverse nature. Beyond typical courier businesses, there are logistics giants, freight forwarders, and e-commerce platforms that provide their own delivery services.

Each of these individuals brings their own set of talents and capabilities to the table, influencing the competitive scene in diverse ways.

For example, logistics behemoths frequently have enormous worldwide networks and cutting-edge technological infrastructure, allowing them to provide full end-to-end solutions for organizations with complicated shipping requirements. Smaller courier businesses, on the other hand, may prioritize agility and customized service, serving specialized markets or geographic areas where bigger players may be underrepresented.

Competition analysis entails investigating the methods and techniques used by these important actors to acquire a competitive advantage. This involves analyzing pricing structures, service offerings, client acquisition and retention methods, as well as technological advancements that improve operational efficiency and customer experience.

Understanding the regulatory environment and market developments is critical for performing a thorough competitive study.

Regulatory changes, such as new transportation legislation or environmental rules, can have a considerable influence on the competitive landscape, influencing important industry participants' strategies and goals. Staying up-to-date on emerging trends and disruptive technology is critical for forecasting changes in the competitive landscape. For example, the emergence of autonomous delivery vehicles, drone delivery services, and the incorporation of artificial intelligence into logistics operations are all variables that have the potential to disrupt existing business models and transform the courier industry's competitive dynamic.

In short, important players and competitive analysis provide essential information for companies attempting to negotiate the difficult landscape of the courier market. Understanding the strengths, weaknesses, and strategies of existing players, as well as staying up-to-date on regulatory changes and emerging trends, allows aspiring entrepreneurs to strategically position themselves to seize opportunities and overcome challenges as they embark on their journey to establish successful courier businesses.

Trends and Future Prospects

Exploring the courier industry's future possibilities and developing trends is like peeking into a crystal ball, seeing glimpses of the revolutionary forces driving the logistics world. This book invites businesses to embark on an exploratory trip, diving into the world of possibilities and innovations that promise to transform the very nature of courier services.

At the core of this future potential is the unstoppable march of technology. From the introduction of self-driving trucks to the incorporation of artificial intelligence and machine learning algorithms into logistical operations, the courier business is on the verge of a technological revolution. Entrepreneurs that are willing to embrace these innovations may open up a world of possibilities, employing cutting-edge technologies to improve efficiency, optimize routes, and provide unmatched client experiences.

The growth of e-commerce will continue to have a significant impact on the future of the courier sector. With more people resorting to online shopping for their daily necessities, the need for speedy and dependable delivery services has increased. Entrepreneurs that place themselves at the intersection of e-commerce and logistics stand to benefit significantly, tapping into a sector ripe for development and expansion. Sustainability appears to be a key trend that will shape the courier industry's future.

As environmental issues gain traction and customers become more environmentally conscious, there is an increasing need for sustainable delivery options that decrease carbon emissions and environmental effects. Entrepreneurs that prioritize sustainability in their operations not only help to make the world a greener place, but they also position themselves as leaders in a market that is becoming increasingly ethical.

In addition to technical improvements and altering customer preferences, geopolitical considerations and global trends influence the courier industry's future. Entrepreneurs must navigate a complex landscape filled with uncertainty and obstacles, encompassing trade agreements, regulatory changes, geopolitical tensions, and economic fluctuations. However, individuals with foresight and agility may transform these obstacles into opportunities, exploiting their insights to remain ahead of the competition and succeed in an ever-changing market climate.

The courier industry's future potential is as large and dynamic as the global marketplace itself. Entrepreneurs who respond to the invitation to explore these possibilities face a landscape ripe for innovation and disruption. By embracing technology improvements, aligning with changing customer tastes, and managing geopolitical intricacies, budding entrepreneurs can trace their own way to success, carving out their own paths through the diverse tapestry of logistics.

Create a Business Plan

Crafting a business strategy is similar to constructing the groundwork for a massive skyscraper, with every element methodically planned to assure its stability and success. In the context of launching a courier service, creating a detailed business plan is more than just a first step in launching a courier service; it's a road map that helps entrepreneurs navigate the complexities of establishing and growing their firm in the changing logistics industry.

A business plan is essentially a roadmap for success, describing the courier firm's vision, objectives, and goals. It contains the entrepreneur's goals, articulates their unique value offer, and establishes a path for development and success.

Entrepreneurs begin the process of establishing a business strategy by conducting extensive market research on industry trends, consumer demographics, and competitive landscapes. Understanding the characteristics of the courier industry and finding areas for differentiation allows entrepreneurs to customize their business strategies to capitalize on market demand and carve out a place in the competitive field.

A business plan also dives into the operational complexities of the courier industry, highlighting logistical factors such as fleet management, route optimization, and technology integration. Entrepreneurs must carefully evaluate their resource needs, ranging from cars and equipment to staff and infrastructure, and design ways to maximize operational efficiency and cost-effectiveness.

Financial planning is another important aspect of the company strategy, in which entrepreneurs predict revenue projections, budget allocations, and financial milestones. Entrepreneurs may reduce possible obstacles by undertaking rigorous financial analysis and risk assessment, laying the framework for long-term development and profitability.

A business plan also includes marketing and sales strategies, which outline how the courier firm will acquire and maintain clients in a competitive market. Entrepreneurs must develop complete plans to boost client acquisition and loyalty, including digital marketing campaigns and smart alliances with e-commerce platforms and local companies.

In addition to establishing strategy and objectives, a business plan is a live document that changes with the company. As entrepreneurs negotiate the courier industry's obstacles and possibilities, they must evaluate and change their business plans on a regular basis in order to respond to changing market dynamics and accomplish their long-term objectives.

Creating a business plan is a critical component of beginning a courier service, providing entrepreneurs with a road map to success in the ever-changing logistics industry. By painstakingly preparing every area of their endeavor, from market analysis and operational logistics to financial forecasts and marketing tactics, entrepreneurs can build the framework for a strong and sustainable courier service that produces results.

The significance of a detailed business strategy.

Crafting a solid business plan is the foundation of every successful company, and it is especially important when beginning a courier business. This document is more than simply a plan; it's a blueprint that includes the vision, tactics, and goals that will help entrepreneurs navigate the difficulties of the courier industry.

A detailed company strategy offers clarity and direction. It requires entrepreneurs to describe their vision for the courier firm, including its mission, goals, and distinct value offer. By putting pen to paper and describing their goals in detail, entrepreneurs obtain a clear grasp of the road they must take to attain success.

A company's plan is a tool for making strategic decisions. Entrepreneurs must undertake rigorous market research, examining industry trends, consumer demographics, and competitive landscapes.

Entrepreneurs may use this information to make educated decisions about their company strategy, including price and service offers, marketing, and operational logistics.

Financial planning is an important component of a comprehensive company strategy. By projecting revenue estimates, budget allocations, and financial milestones, entrepreneurs may guarantee that their courier service is financially viable and sustainable in the long term. Additionally, financial planning assists entrepreneurs in identifying possible risks and obstacles, allowing them to create methods to manage these risks and protect their company's financial health.

In addition, a detailed company plan functions as a communication tool. Whether entrepreneurs are looking for investor finance or collaborations with suppliers and vendors, a well-written business plan may successfully communicate the courier service's value offer and development potential. It builds trust among stakeholders and sets the framework for effective collaborations that may move the business ahead.

A complete company plan not only provides clarity, strategic direction, financial planning, and communication, but it also acts as a road map for future progress. As the courier industry grows and adapts to shifting market circumstances, entrepreneurs can look back on their business plan to realign their strategy and goals accordingly. It becomes a living document that grows alongside the company, directing its course toward long-term success.

The value of developing a detailed business strategy when launching a courier service cannot be overemphasized. It gives clarity, strategic direction, financial planning, communication, and a strategy for future development and expansion. Entrepreneurs that create a well-thought-out business strategy build the framework for a successful endeavor in the dynamic and competitive courier sector.

Legal and Regulatory Considerations

When venturing into the arena of founding a courier service, entrepreneurs must navigate a maze of legal and regulatory concerns that form the face of the sector. From transportation rules to data protection standards, understanding and complying with these criteria are vital for ensuring the success and sustainability of the endeavor. At the forefront of legal and regulatory issues is conformity to transportation rules and regulations. The courier sector operates within a network of rules controlling the movement of goods, vehicles, and drivers. Entrepreneurs must educate themselves with these rules, which may vary depending on the jurisdiction, and ensure that their activities conform to requirements such as vehicle safety standards, driver license and certification, and insurance coverage. By conforming to transportation rules, businesses may reduce legal risks, preserve their assets, and guarantee the safety and well-being of their employees and consumers.

Moreover, data protection standards play a key role in the courier sector, particularly in the age of digitization and e-commerce. As courier firms acquire and use customer data for reasons such as order monitoring and delivery notifications, they must adhere to data protection laws and regulations to ensure consumer privacy and prevent data breaches. Entrepreneurs must implement robust data protection measures, such as encryption protocols, secure data storage, and access controls, to ensure compliance with regulations such as the General Data Protection Regulation (GDPR) in the European Union or the California Consumer Privacy Act (CCPA) in the United States. By emphasizing data safety and privacy, entrepreneurs may create confidence and credibility with clients and minimize legal risks related to data breaches. Legal and regulatory issues extend to areas like taxes, employment law, and environmental rules. Entrepreneurs must understand their tax obligations, including income tax, sales tax, and payroll tax, and maintain compliance with tax laws and regulations to avoid penalties and legal concerns.

Additionally, entrepreneurs must also comply with employment regulations covering factors such as recruiting methods, employee benefits, and workplace safety to establish a healthy and compliant work environment. Moreover, environmental rules may harm courier firms, particularly those involved in the delivery of hazardous items or operating in ecologically sensitive locations. Entrepreneurs must understand and comply with environmental standards to reduce their environmental imprint and avoid legal liabilities associated with environmental infractions.

In essence, legal and regulatory issues are important to the success and longevity of a courier service. Understanding and complying with transportation laws, data protection regulations, taxation requirements, employment laws, and environmental regulations, entrepreneurs can mitigate legal risks, protect their assets, and build a compliant and resilient business that thrives in the competitive landscape of the courier industry.

Registering your courier business

On starting the adventure of launching a courier service, one of the most important tasks is registering the business entity with the appropriate authorities. Registering your courier service is not only a legal obligation but also a crucial step towards creating legitimacy, trust, and accountability in the eyes of clients, suppliers, and other stakeholders.

The process of establishing your courier service begins with picking an appropriate business structure. Entrepreneurs have several alternatives, including sole proprietorship, partnership, limited liability company (LLC), or corporation. Each business structure has its own set of advantages and drawbacks in terms of liability protection, tax ramifications, and administrative requirements. Entrepreneurs must carefully examine these aspects and pick the business structure that best matches their aims and preferences.

Entrepreneurs must register their courier business with the necessary government authorities at the local, state, and federal levels once they have decided on the business structure. This often requires acquiring a business license or permission from the local municipality or county where the business operates.

Additionally, depending on the nature of the courier business and the services provided, entrepreneurs may need to obtain specific permissions or licenses from regulatory authorities, such as a transportation or delivery license. Entrepreneurs must register their courier firm with the state government to get a unique tax identification number or employer identification number (EIN). This number is crucial for filing taxes, creating company bank accounts, and recruiting personnel. Furthermore, if the courier service operates under a fake or "doing business as" (DBA) name, entrepreneurs must register this name with the appropriate state or county authorities to ensure legal compliance.

In addition to registering with government organizations, entrepreneurs may also need to earn certain industry-specific qualifications or affiliations to operate their courier service lawfully and professionally. For example, courier companies involved in the delivery of hazardous chemicals may need to seek hazardous material transportation certification from regulatory authorities. Similarly, courier organizations that offer specialist services, such as medical or pharmaceutical delivery, may need to obtain industry-specific certificates or affiliations to demonstrate proficiency and compliance with industry norms.

Registering your courier service is a vital step toward establishing legality, reliability, and responsibility in the competitive landscape of the courier sector. By choosing a suitable business structure, obtaining the necessary licenses and permits, registering with government agencies, and obtaining industry-specific certifications or memberships, entrepreneurs can ensure legal compliance and lay the groundwork for a successful and sustainable courier business venture.

Understanding licenses and permits

Knowing licenses and permissions when launching a courier service is equivalent to unlocking the key to legitimacy and compliance within the regulatory landscape. It's a key facet that entrepreneurs must negotiate to ensure their operations conform to regulatory regulations and industry norms while also establishing trust and credibility with consumers and stakeholders.

Licenses and permits comprise a broad spectrum of governmental permissions and authorizations that control many parts of the courier company. From corporate licenses and operating permits to industry-specific certificates and registrations, each serves a different role in ensuring compliance with applicable laws and regulations.

At the onset, entrepreneurs must seek a business license or permission from the local government authority in the territory where the courier firm works. This license acts as a fundamental authority to conduct business lawfully within the region and is often necessary for all sorts of enterprises, including courier services. It establishes the corporate entity's legal identification and denotes its compliance with local legislation and tax requirements. Moreover, depending on the nature of the courier business and the services provided, entrepreneurs may need to seek specific permissions or licenses from regulatory organizations at the local, state, or federal levels. For example, courier companies involved in product delivery may need to obtain transit permits or operational licenses from regulatory bodies controlling transportation and logistics. Similarly, courier services that operate cars for commercial purposes may need to obtain commercial vehicle permits or licenses to ensure compliance with vehicle safety standards and laws.

The knowledge of licenses and permissions extends to industry-specific certificates and registrations that may be required to operate a courier service lawfully and credibly. For example, courier services that handle hazardous items or medical supplies may need to get specialist certificates or registrations to demonstrate compliance with industry norms and laws. Likewise, courier firms that operate abroad may need to get customs and import/export permits to allow cross-border transportation and maintain compliance with international trade rules.

To acquiring licenses and permits, entrepreneurs must also maintain compliance with regulatory requirements by renewing licenses and permits as necessary and being aware of changes in legislation that may affect their operations. Failure to comply with licensing and permitting regulations can result in legal penalties, fines, or even suspension of operations, compromising the viability and sustainability of the courier service.

Compliance with transportation regulations

Stepping into the field of launching a courier service, one must traverse a maze of transportation rules to ensure compliance and operational success. These laws, set out by different governmental agencies, are aimed at ensuring safety standards, safeguarding public welfare, and maintaining order within the transportation industry.

Vehicle safety requirements are at the forefront of compliance with transportation legislation. Courier firms rely significantly on their fleet of trucks to convey products efficiently and reliably. As such, ensuring that these cars fulfill safety requirements imposed by regulatory agencies is vital. This may comprise frequent vehicle inspections, maintenance checks, and adherence to safety standards to limit hazards and prevent accidents on the road.

Moreover, compliance with transportation legislation extends to driver's license and certification requirements. Courier firms must verify that their drivers have the proper credentials and certificates to operate commercial vehicles legally. This may entail getting commercial driver's licenses (CDLs), attending specific training programs, and following standards controlling driver conduct and safety procedures while on the road.

These firms must conform to standards controlling the delivery of products, particularly if they handle specialized or dangerous commodities. This may entail acquiring permissions or licenses for the transportation of certain types of commodities, following packing and labeling standards, and adhering to rules controlling the handling and storage of hazardous items to guarantee public safety and environmental protection. In addition to vehicle and driver compliance, courier firms must also manage rules governing operational logistics and commercial operations. This may involve conforming to rules controlling delivery timetables, service standards, and customer contacts, as well as maintaining correct records and paperwork to provide openness and accountability in business operations.

Compliance with transportation rules is not only a legal requirement; it's a commitment to safety, honesty, and professionalism within the courier sector. Emphasizing compliance with transportation standards, courier services may create trust and credibility with customers, suppliers, and stakeholders, building a favorable reputation and positioning themselves for success in the competitive marketplace.

In essence, compliance with transportation standards is a core part of launching and managing a courier service. By ensuring adherence to vehicle safety standards, driver licensing and certification requirements, regulations governing the transportation of goods, and operational logistics, courier businesses can uphold safety standards, protect public welfare, and maintain order within the transportation industry, positioning themselves for success and sustainability in the competitive landscape of logistics.

Insurance requirements and liability protection

As entrepreneurs embark on the exciting path of launching a courier service, they must traverse a tangle of insurance regulations and liability concerns to safeguard their assets, employees, and clients. In the volatile environment of the courier business, insurance acts as a key safety net, giving financial security and peace of mind in the case of unanticipated accidents, mishaps, or litigation.

At the forefront of the insurance requirements for a courier service is commercial auto insurance. Given that courier services rely largely on their fleet of cars to convey products and perform deliveries, having proper commercial auto insurance coverage is vital. This sort of insurance covers against losses or injuries stemming from incidents involving corporate cars, including bodily injury liability, property damage liability, and collision coverage. Moreover, depending on the nature of the courier service and the types of items delivered, extra coverage choices such as cargo insurance may be essential to safeguard against loss or damage to goods during transit.

Courier services must also consider liability insurance to safeguard against any lawsuits or claims originating from accidents, injuries, or property damage. General liability insurance provides coverage for third-party bodily injury or property damage claims that may arise on company premises or as a result of business operations. Additionally, professional liability insurance, often known as errors and omissions insurance, may be essential to safeguard against claims of carelessness, mistakes, or omissions in the execution of courier services.

Furthermore, courier firms' insurance requirements extend beyond physical asset protection and liability considerations to include personnel coverage. Workers' compensation insurance is vital for providing financial security and medical benefits to employees who experience work-related accidents or illnesses. State laws and regulations often mandate this insurance, which helps cover medical expenditures, missed income, and rehabilitation costs for injured employees.

In addition to acquiring insurance coverage, courier firms must also consider liability protection through legal structures such as limited liability companies (LLCs) or corporations. These legal structures provide protection for personal assets and minimize the responsibility of business owners in the case of lawsuits or claims against the business. By forming a distinct legal corporation for the courier service, entrepreneurs may preserve their own assets and shield themselves from personal accountability for business debts or legal responsibilities.

Insurance requirements and liability protection are key concerns for entrepreneurs beginning a courier service. By securing adequate insurance coverage, including commercial auto insurance, liability insurance, and workers' compensation insurance, and considering liability protection through legal entities, entrepreneurs can protect their assets, employees, and customers, mitigate risks, and ensure the long-term success and sustainability of their courier business venture.

Establishing Operations

Setting up operations for a courier business is similar to orchestrating a symphony, with each component working together to provide a seamless and efficient delivery experience to customers. Establishing logistical frameworks and implementing technology solutions requires a meticulous blend of strategic planning, resource allocation, and operational execution to ensure the courier business runs smoothly.

One of the first steps in establishing operations is to define a logistical framework that will support the delivery process. This includes determining service areas, delivery zones, and pickup and drop-off points. Courier businesses can improve efficiency, reduce delivery times, and increase customer satisfaction by strategically mapping service areas and delivery routes. Furthermore, establishing clear protocols for pickup and drop-off procedures ensures seamless coordination among drivers, customers, and delivery locations, thereby improving the overall customer experience.

In addition to defining the logistical framework, setting up operations entails assembling a dependable and efficient fleet of vehicles to make deliveries. This includes selecting appropriate vehicles based on delivery size and type, ensuring vehicle maintenance and safety inspections, and implementing real-time tracking systems. Courier businesses can improve fleet management, operational efficiency, and delivery reliability by investing in well-maintained vehicles and leveraging technology solutions such as GPS tracking.

Establishing operations entails creating strong systems and processes to streamline day-to-day operations and ensure consistent service quality. This includes implementing software solutions for order management, route optimization, and driver dispatching, as well as developing protocols for order tracking, customer communication, and problem resolution. Using technology and automation tools, courier companies can streamline operations, improve workflow efficiency, and improve the overall customer experience.

Setting up operations entails forming partnerships and collaborations with suppliers, vendors, and service providers to help with the delivery process. This includes sourcing packaging materials, securing transportation for long-distance deliveries, and collaborating with logistics providers for specialized services like international shipping or temperature-controlled transport. Courier businesses can increase their competitive advantage in the marketplace by forming strong partnerships and collaborations.

Additionally, starting operations entails hiring and training a skilled team of employees to handle various aspects of the delivery process. This includes hiring drivers, customer service representatives, and operational personnel, as well as offering comprehensive training programs to ensure adherence to safety standards, customer service protocols, and operational procedures. By investing in employee training and development, courier businesses can create a capable and competent workforce that provides exceptional service while maintaining the company's reputation for dependability and professionalism.

Establishing operations for a courier business is a multifaceted endeavor that includes defining logistical frameworks, building a dependable fleet of vehicles, implementing technology solutions, developing robust systems and processes, forming partnerships and collaborations, and hiring and training skilled employees. By carefully orchestrating these components, entrepreneurs can lay the groundwork for a successful and efficient courier business that provides value to customers while driving long-term growth and sustainability.

Selecting the appropriate location for your business

Finding the ideal location for a courier business is similar to finding the perfect setting for a masterpiece painting: it lays the groundwork for success and provides the foundation for the business to grow. A courier business's location has a significant impact on its operational efficiency, customer accessibility, and overall market competitiveness.

Entrepreneurs must consider the geographical landscape when determining the best location for their courier business. Factors like proximity to major transportation routes, highways, and logistical hubs are critical for optimizing delivery routes and reducing transit times.

A centrally located facility with easy access to major highways and transportation arteries can significantly improve the efficiency of courier business operations, allowing for timely and cost-effective deliveries to customers.

When deciding on a location for their courier business, entrepreneurs must also consider the area's demographics.

Understanding the local population density, demographic composition, and economic profile is critical for identifying potential customer segments and courier service demand. For example, a densely populated urban area with a high concentration of businesses and residential complexes may provide a profitable market for courier services, whereas a rural area with dispersed population centers may present different opportunities and challenges.

When deciding on the best location for their courier business, entrepreneurs must consider not only geography and demographics but also the competitive landscape. Analyzing the presence of competing courier services, logistical infrastructure, and customer preferences in the region can provide useful information about market dynamics and potential differentiation opportunities.

Entrepreneurs can carve out a market niche and attract customers looking for dependable and efficient courier services by strategically positioning their business in a location that gives them a competitive advantage.

Entrepreneurs must consider the availability of suitable facilities and infrastructure when choosing a location for their courier business. Access to commercial space, parking facilities, and loading docks is critical for facilitating day-to-day operations and meeting the logistics needs of the courier industry.

Factors such as proximity to suppliers, vendors, and service providers can improve operational efficiency and speed up the delivery process.

Entrepreneurs must also consider regulatory and zoning requirements when determining the best location for their courier business. Ensuring compliance with local zoning laws, building codes, and regulatory requirements is critical for obtaining necessary permits and licenses and avoiding legal issues that could impede the business's operation. By conducting extensive due diligence and consulting with legal and regulatory experts, entrepreneurs can navigate the complexities of regulatory compliance and choose a location that aligns with their business goals and objectives.

Determining the best location for a courier business is a strategic decision that must take into account geographical, demographic, competitive, infrastructural, and regulatory factors. Entrepreneurs can lay the groundwork for a successful and thriving courier business by evaluating these factors and choosing a location that provides optimal accessibility, market potential, competitive advantage, and regulatory compliance.

Developing operational processes and workflows.

Establishing operational processes and workflows is the foundation of a successful courier business, similar to laying the tracks for a high-speed train to travel smoothly through the logistics landscape. It entails creating efficient and systematic procedures that govern all aspects of the delivery process, from order intake to final delivery, in order to ensure peak performance, customer satisfaction, and business success.

The goal of establishing operational processes and workflows is to streamline order intake and processing. This involves implementing user-friendly systems for customers to place orders, whether it be through online platforms, mobile applications, or traditional phone calls. By providing multiple channels for order placement and ensuring seamless integration with backend systems, courier businesses can efficiently capture and process orders, minimizing delays and errors in the order intake process.

Moreover, establishing operational processes and workflows involves optimizing route planning and dispatching procedures.

This includes leveraging technology solutions such as route optimization software, GPS tracking systems, and real-time traffic updates to optimize delivery routes, minimize travel times, and maximize the efficiency of driver dispatching.

Automating route planning and dispatching processes, courier businesses can improve operational efficiency, reduce fuel costs, and enhance the reliability of delivery services.

However, establishing operational processes and workflows entails developing robust systems for package handling and tracking. This includes implementing barcode scanning systems, RFID technology, and electronic signature capture to track the movement of packages throughout the delivery process accurately. By providing real-time visibility into package locations and delivery statuses, courier businesses can enhance transparency, accountability, and customer satisfaction, reducing the risk of lost or delayed shipments.

In addition to optimizing order intake, route planning, and package handling processes, establishing operational processes and workflows involves developing comprehensive protocols for customer communication and issue resolution.

This includes providing timely updates and notifications to customers regarding order status, delivery times, and any unforeseen delays or issues that may arise during the delivery process. By maintaining open lines of communication and proactively addressing customer concerns, courier businesses can build trust, loyalty, and satisfaction among their customer base.

Establishing operational processes and workflows extends to developing protocols for driver training and performance management. This includes providing comprehensive training programs for drivers on safety procedures, customer service standards, and operational protocols, as well as implementing performance metrics and feedback mechanisms to monitor driver performance and ensure compliance with company policies and standards.

In essence, establishing operational processes and workflows is a multifaceted endeavor that involves streamlining order intake, optimizing route planning and dispatching, implementing package handling and tracking systems, developing customer communication protocols, and providing driver training and performance management.

Procuring necessary equipment and vehicles

Procuring necessary equipment and vehicles is akin to assembling the tools of the trade for a courier business, essential for navigating the complex logistics terrain and delivering exceptional service to customers. From vehicles to technology solutions, each piece of equipment plays a crucial role in ensuring the efficiency, reliability, and success of the courier business operation.

At the forefront of procuring necessary equipment and vehicles is the selection of an appropriate fleet of vehicles. Vehicles are the lifeline of a courier business, serving as the means to transport goods and fulfill deliveries efficiently and reliably. Entrepreneurs must carefully consider factors such as vehicle size, capacity, and specifications based on types of deliveries and service areas. Whether it's vans, trucks, bicycles, or motorcycles, selecting the right mix of vehicles ensures that the courier business can meet the diverse needs of customers while optimizing operational efficiency and cost-effectiveness. Moreover, procuring necessary equipment extends beyond vehicles to include technology solutions that enhance operational efficiency and the customer experience. This may include investing in delivery management software, GPS tracking systems, and mobile applications that streamline order management, route planning, and driver dispatching. By leveraging technology solutions, courier businesses can automate repetitive tasks, improve workflow efficiency, and provide real-time visibility into delivery statuses, enhancing the overall customer experience and service quality.

Procuring the necessary equipment and vehicles involves ensuring compliance with safety and regulatory standards. This includes equipping vehicles with safety features such as GPS tracking devices, backup cameras, and vehicle safety kits to ensure driver safety and compliance with transportation regulations. Additionally, vehicles may need to undergo regular maintenance checks, safety inspections, and compliance audits to ensure optimal performance and adherence to safety standards.

In addition to vehicles and technology solutions, procuring necessary equipment may also entail sourcing packaging materials, shipping supplies, and logistical equipment required for the delivery process. Shipping labels, packaging tape, dunnage materials, and handling equipment may be included to facilitate safe and efficient handling of packages and goods during transit. By procuring high-quality packaging materials and logistical equipment, courier businesses can ensure the integrity and security of shipments while minimizing the risk of damage or loss.

Moreover, procuring the necessary equipment and vehicles requires careful financial planning and resource allocation. Entrepreneurs must consider factors such as budget constraints, financing options, and the total cost of ownership when acquiring vehicles and equipment for their courier business.

Whether it's purchasing vehicles outright, leasing vehicles, or exploring financing options, entrepreneurs must evaluate the long-term costs and benefits of each option to make informed decisions that align with their business goals and objectives.

In essence, procuring necessary equipment and vehicles is a strategic investment that lays the foundation for the success and sustainability of a courier business. Selecting an appropriate fleet of vehicles, investing in technology solutions, ensuring compliance with safety and regulatory standards, sourcing high-quality packaging materials, and conducting careful financial planning, entrepreneurs can equip their courier business with the tools and resources necessary to deliver exceptional service and thrive in the competitive landscape of logistics.

Hiring and training staff

In building a successful courier business, hiring and training staff are crucial steps in ensuring the smooth operation and delivery of exceptional service to customers. Employees of a courier business are more than just workers; they are the company's face, the backbone of its operations, and the key to its success. As such, recruiting and training the right individuals is paramount to creating a competent and reliable workforce that can meet the demands of the dynamic courier industry.

The hiring process for a courier business begins with identifying the specific roles and responsibilities needed to support the operation. This may include drivers for vehicle operation, customer service representatives for order management and communication, and operational staff for warehouse management and logistics coordination. Each role requires a unique set of skills, qualifications, and attributes to perform effectively within the fast-paced and demanding environment of a courier business.

When recruiting staff, courier businesses must prioritize qualities such as reliability, attention to detail, and a strong work ethic. Drivers, in particular, must possess excellent driving skills, a clean driving record, and the ability to navigate efficiently through various routes and traffic conditions. Customer service representatives should have strong communication skills, problem-solving abilities, and a customer-centric approach to handle inquiries, complaints, and requests effectively. Operational staff must be organized, detail-oriented, and capable of managing logistics, inventory, and warehouse operations with precision and efficiency.

Moreover, hiring staff for a courier business involves conducting thorough interviews, background checks, and reference checks to assess candidates' qualifications, experience, and suitability for the role. This includes evaluating candidates' knowledge of transportation regulations, familiarity with local geography, and experience in customer service or logistics-related roles. By conducting rigorous screening and selection processes, courier businesses can ensure that they hire individuals who are not only qualified but also aligned with the company's values, culture, and vision.

Once the right individuals have been hired, training becomes essential to equipping employees with the knowledge, skills, and resources necessary to perform their roles effectively. Training programs for drivers may include instruction on safe driving practices, defensive driving techniques, and vehicle maintenance procedures to ensure compliance with safety standards and regulations. Customer service representatives may receive training on order management systems, communication protocols, and conflict resolution techniques to deliver exceptional service and resolve customer issues promptly and professionally. Operational staff may undergo training on warehouse management systems, inventory control procedures, and logistical processes to optimize efficiency and accuracy in warehouse operations and order fulfillment.

Furthermore, ongoing training and development are essential to keep employees updated on industry trends, technological advancements, and best practices in the courier industry.

This may include providing access to training resources, workshops, and seminars to enhance employees' skills and knowledge and promote continuous improvement and professional growth. Courier businesses can cultivate a skilled and motivated workforce, enabling them to adapt to changing market dynamics, meet evolving customer needs, and drive the success and growth of the business through investing in employee training and development.

In summary, hiring and training staff are critical components of building a successful courier business. By recruiting individuals with the right qualifications, skills, and attributes, conducting thorough screening and selection processes, and providing comprehensive training and development programs, courier businesses can build a competent and reliable workforce that delivers exceptional service, upholds the company's reputation, and drives long-term success in the competitive landscape of logistics.

Building Partnerships and Networks

Building partnerships and networks is a cornerstone of success in the courier business, akin to weaving a web of interconnected relationships that support and strengthen the operation. In the dynamic and competitive landscape of logistics, forging strategic partnerships and cultivating robust networks is essential for expanding service offerings, accessing new markets, and enhancing operational efficiency and effectiveness.

At the heart of building partnerships and networks is establishing collaborative relationships with suppliers, vendors, and service providers. Courier businesses rely on a wide range of suppliers for essential materials and services, including packaging materials, shipping supplies, vehicle maintenance, and logistical support. By cultivating strong partnerships with reliable suppliers, courier businesses can ensure a steady supply of high-quality materials and services, optimize procurement processes, and reduce costs through bulk purchasing agreements and favorable terms.

Moreover, building partnerships and networks involves establishing alliances with other players in the logistics ecosystem, including transportation companies, freight forwarders, and warehousing facilities.

Collaboration with transportation companies enables courier businesses to broaden their service offerings, access new markets, and leverage additional transportation capacity to meet customer demand. Similarly, partnering with freight forwarders and warehousing facilities enables courier businesses to tap into additional logistical capabilities, such as international shipping, storage, and distribution services, to enhance their value proposition and competitive advantage in the market.

In building partnerships and networks, it entails forging alliances with complementary businesses and industry stakeholders. This may include partnering with e-commerce platforms, retailers, and manufacturers to provide last-mile delivery services for their products, facilitating faster delivery times and greater convenience for customers. Additionally, collaborating with technology providers, software developers, and IT solutions companies allows courier businesses to leverage cutting-edge technology solutions, such as delivery management software, route optimization tools, and GPS tracking systems, to improve operational efficiency, enhance the customer experience, and stay ahead of the competition.

In addition to establishing external partnerships, building partnerships and networks also involves nurturing relationships with internal stakeholders, including employees, drivers, and subcontractors. By fostering a culture of collaboration, communication, and teamwork within the organization, courier businesses can enhance employee morale, productivity, and job satisfaction, leading to higher levels of customer satisfaction and business success. Moreover, cultivating strong relationships with drivers and subcontractors ensures a reliable and flexible workforce that can meet fluctuating demand and adapt to changing market conditions effectively.

Building partnerships and networks involves actively engaging with industry associations, trade organizations, and professional networks to stay informed about industry trends, best practices, and regulatory developments. Participating in industry events, conferences, and forums provides opportunities for networking, knowledge sharing, and collaboration with peers and industry experts, enabling courier businesses to stay ahead of the curve, identify emerging opportunities, and navigate challenges effectively.

In essence, building partnerships and networks is a strategic imperative for success in the courier business. In forging collaborative relationships with suppliers, vendors, and service providers, partnering with other players in the logistics ecosystem, collaborating with complementary businesses and industry stakeholders, nurturing internal relationships, and engaging with industry associations and professional networks, courier businesses can expand their service offerings, access new markets, enhance operational efficiency, and drive long-term growth and success in the competitive landscape of logistics.

Establishing relationships with clients and vendors

Establishing relationships with clients and vendors is the cornerstone of success in the courier business, akin to laying the foundation for a thriving ecosystem of partnerships and collaborations. In the dynamic and competitive landscape of logistics, building strong and enduring relationships with clients and vendors is essential for fostering trust, loyalty, and mutual support, ultimately driving the growth and success of the courier business.

At the heart of establishing relationships with clients is understanding their unique needs, preferences, and expectations. Courier businesses must take a customer-centric approach, listening attentively to clients' requirements and tailoring their services to meet and exceed their expectations. By demonstrating a deep understanding of clients' businesses, industries, and logistical challenges, courier businesses can build credibility, rapport, and trust with clients, industries, and logistical challenges. This lays the groundwork for long-term partnerships and repeat business.

Creating relationships with clients involves providing exceptional service and delivering on promises consistently. Reliability, timeliness, and accuracy must be the top priorities for courier businesses in their delivery services to ensure shipments are handled with care, delivered on time, and arrive in perfect condition. By delivering exceptional service experiences, courier businesses can earn clients' trust and confidence, foster loyalty and retention, and secure a competitive edge in the market.

Establishing relationships with clients extends beyond transactional interactions to proactive communication and relationship management.

Courier businesses must maintain open lines of communication with clients, providing timely updates, notifications, and proactive solutions to address any issues or concerns that may arise during the delivery process. In addition to establishing relationships with clients, building relationships with vendors is equally important for the success of a courier business.

Vendors play a critical role in supporting the operations of courier businesses, providing essential materials, services, and logistical support necessary for delivering exceptional service to clients. Courier businesses must prioritize building strong and collaborative relationships with vendors and fostering mutual trust, respect, and reliability.

Establishing relationships with vendors involves selecting reputable and reliable suppliers who can meet the quality, quantity, and timeliness requirements of the courier business. In businesses must conduct thorough due diligence and vetting processes to evaluate vendors' capabilities, track record, and adherence to quality and compliance standards. By partnering with trusted vendors, courier businesses can ensure a steady supply of high-quality materials and services, minimize risks, and optimize procurement processes.

Moreover, establishing relationships with vendors entails effective communication, negotiation, and collaboration to achieve mutual goals and objectives. Courier businesses must maintain open lines of communication with vendors, providing clear expectations, specifications, and feedback to ensure alignment and accountability. By fostering a collaborative partnership approach, courier businesses can work closely with vendors to address challenges, explore opportunities, and drive continuous improvement in their operations.

Building a lasting relationship with vendors involves cultivating a culture of partnership and mutual support where vendors are viewed as valued collaborators rather than mere suppliers. Courier businesses must prioritize fairness, integrity, and transparency in their dealings with vendors, treating them with respect and appreciation for their contributions to the success of the business.

Negotiating contracts and service agreements

Negotiating contracts and service agreements is an important element of beginning and sustaining a successful courier business, as it lays the groundwork for mutually beneficial relationships with clients and providers. These contracts and agreements establish the foundation for the terms, conditions, and expectations of the business partnership, guaranteeing clarity, transparency, and responsibility for all parties involved.

Understanding both parties' needs, requirements, and expectations is crucial to contract and service agreement negotiations. For courier companies, this means undertaking detailed assessments of clients' logistical demands, delivery preferences, and service level expectations. Similarly, vendors and service providers must assess their capabilities, experience, and ability to satisfy the needs of the courier industry.

Understanding each party's specific demands and objectives allows courier firms to adjust their products and negotiate conditions that are mutually advantageous and consistent with both parties' aims.

Writing contracts and service agreements requires balancing customer expectations with the courier business's profitability and viability. Pricing, payment terms, service levels, and performance measures are all important considerations.

Courier firms must examine the service delivery expenses, including labor, fuel, maintenance, and overhead, and establish pricing structures that are both competitive and profitable. Creating clear payment conditions, incentives, and penalties for noncompliance helps to limit risks and assure timely payments, thus improving the financial stability of the courier industry.

When drafting contracts and service agreements, it is necessary to clearly and specifically outline the areas of services, obligations, and deliverables. Specify the services to be provided, along with the delivery frequency and schedule, and any additional services or value-added products. In addition to defining the scope of services, negotiating contracts and service agreements includes developing performance metrics and key performance indicators (KPIs) to assess and evaluate the quality and efficiency of service delivery.

This might include measures like on-time delivery performance, delivery accuracy, customer satisfaction ratings, and service level agreement (SLA) compliance. Setting defined performance objectives and standards allows courier firms to track their performance, identify areas for development, and maintain accountability and openness in the business relationship.

Writing contracts and service agreements necessitates including measures for flexibility and adaptability to changing conditions. In the fast-paced and dynamic logistics industry, unanticipated occurrences, such as changes in market conditions, regulatory requirements, or client needs, may necessitate contract adjustments. Courier firms must include modification, revision, and termination terms that allow for flexibility and adaptability to new conditions while preserving both parties' interests.

Utilizing technology to streamline operations.

In today's fast-paced and highly competitive corporate environment, utilizing technology is critical for attaining efficient operations and staying ahead of the competition. Technology is critical for courier firms because it optimizes procedures, improves the client experience, and drives growth and profitability.

Delivery management software is one way for courier organizations to embrace technology. This software automates and centralizes several components of the delivery process, such as order administration, route planning, and real-time delivery tracking. Courier firms may use delivery management software to effectively manage orders, assign drivers to routes, and track deliveries' progress in real time. This not only increases operational efficiency but also provides clients and customers with greater visibility and transparency by allowing them to trace their goods from pickup to delivery.

Courier firms use technology to streamline route planning and scheduling. Route optimization software uses algorithms to determine the most effective routes for vehicles based on parameters such as traffic conditions, delivery window availability, and fuel efficiency. Optimizing routes, courier companies can reduce fuel costs and travel time while increasing on-time delivery performance. This not only improves operational efficiency, but it also increases customer satisfaction by ensuring timely and consistent delivery.

In addition to route optimization, courier companies utilize technology to improve communication and collaboration among team members. Mobile communication applications and messaging systems enable drivers, dispatchers, and operational personnel to connect in real time, exchange updates, and coordinate actions effortlessly. This improves communication and collaboration, lowers mistakes and delays, and increases overall operational efficiency. Technology helps courier companies provide value-added services while improving the consumer experience. For example, electronic signature capture devices allow drivers to gather signatures digitally upon delivery, eliminating the need for paper-based delivery evidence and expediting the documentation process. Similarly, GPS tracking systems notify clients and customers in real time of the location and status of their goods, increasing transparency and visibility throughout the delivery process.

Technology is critical to data management and analysis in courier firms. Advanced analytics software enables courier firms to examine data on delivery performance, client preferences, and operational efficiency. By evaluating this data, courier companies may uncover trends, patterns, and areas for development, allowing them to make more informed decisions and optimize their operations for improved efficiency and profitability.

Additionally, courier firms use technology to improve security and compliance in their operations. Electronic logging devices (ELDs), for example, serve to guarantee compliance with legislation controlling driver hours and rest intervals, therefore boosting safety and lowering the chance of infringement. Similarly, video surveillance systems and telematics technologies allow courier organizations to monitor driver behavior, vehicle performance, and adherence to safety rules, therefore improving fleet security and compliance.

Using technology is critical for optimizing operations and generating success in the courier industry. Using delivery management software, route optimization tools, mobile communication apps, electronic signature capture devices, GPS tracking systems, analytics software, and other technological innovations, courier businesses can streamline processes, improve productivity, improve customer experience, and remain competitive in the fast-paced world of logistics.

Establishing a solid network of delivery partners.

Creating a dependable network of delivery partners is critical to the success and expansion of a courier service. In the competitive logistics scene, developing strong partnerships with reliable delivery partners is critical for extending service coverage, fulfilling customer demand, and providing great service.

Identifying and establishing a dependable network of delivery partners. Courier organizations must perform extensive research to find reliable delivery providers and independent contractors that share their values, service standards, and operational needs. This might include assessing aspects such as reputation, track record, coverage region, fleet size, and service options.

To create partnerships, courier firms must develop communication and collaboration channels after identifying possible delivery partners. This includes contacting potential partners to establish common goals, expectations, and conditions of involvement. Courier companies must properly express their service needs, performance goals, and key performance indicators (KPIs) to maintain alignment and responsibility.

Building a dependable network of delivery partners necessitates cultivating trust and dependability through honest and open communication. Courier firms must communicate regularly with their delivery partners, offering updates, sharing pertinent information, and addressing any issues or concerns that may emerge. Courier firms can build trust and strengthen relationships with their delivery partners by cultivating a culture of openness and collaboration, which increases service dependability and effectiveness.

Courier organizations must establish clear and mutually beneficial contractual arrangements to build a dependable network of delivery partners.

Courier organizations must negotiate and complete contracts that define the partnership's terms, conditions, and expectations, such as price, service standards, performance benchmarks, and dispute resolution processes. Clear contractual arrangements may help courier organizations reduce risks, assure responsibility, and defend their interests in the collaboration.

In addition to contractual agreements, building a trusted network of delivery partners necessitates continuous performance monitoring and evaluation. Courier companies must monitor and evaluate key performance indicators (KPIs) for delivery partner performance, such as on-time delivery rates, delivery accuracy, customer satisfaction ratings, and adherence to service level agreements (SLAs). By tracking performance indicators, courier companies may discover areas for development, give feedback, and help their delivery partners deliver great service. Building a dependable network of delivery partners necessitates investments in technology and infrastructure to improve communication, cooperation, and coordination.

Courier companies may use delivery management software, route optimization tools, and mobile communication applications to streamline procedures, increase productivity, and improve visibility throughout their network of delivery partners. Investing in technology and infrastructure allows courier services to streamline operations and provide consumers with a seamless and dependable service experience.

Marketing and Branding Strategy

Marketing and branding strategies are critical to building a strong presence and driving development in today's competitive courier industry. In a sector where dependability, efficiency, and customer service are critical, successful marketing and branding initiatives may set a courier company apart, attract customers, and develop long-term connections.

Creating a captivating brand identity is an important part of effective courier marketing and branding strategies. This entails creating a brand story, a mission, and values that resonate with the intended audience. Courier firms may separate themselves from competition by expressing a distinct and appealing brand identity.

A good courier marketing and branding techniques include developing a strong visual identity using branding components like logos, color schemes, and design aesthetics. A visually appealing and unified brand design helps courier firms stand out in a congested field while also increasing brand awareness and recall among clients and consumers.

Also, a courier company's marketing and branding tactics include creating a comprehensive marketing plan that uses a combination of online and offline channels to reach and engage the intended audience. This might involve digital marketing methods like search engine optimization (SEO), social media marketing, email marketing, and pay-per-click (PPC) advertising, as well as classic marketing tactics like print advertising, direct mail, and networking events.

In addition to digital and conventional marketing approaches, effective courier marketing and branding strategies include developing connections with important industry players and influencers. This might involve working with e-commerce platforms, merchants, manufacturers, and other companies that use courier services to reach their consumers.

The courier company's marketing and branding strategies include providing excellent customer service and using consumer feedback and testimonials to increase trust and reputation. Positive word-of-mouth recommendations and testimonials from satisfied clients and customers may be effective marketing techniques for attracting new clients and improving the courier business's industry reputation. A successful marketing and branding strategies for a courier firm must stay current on industry trends, market dynamics, and client preferences in order to adjust and evolve marketing plans accordingly. This may include performing market research, researching rival strategies, and staying current on developing technologies and advances in the logistics business.

Creating a distinctive brand identity

Developing a distinct brand identity is critical for a courier company to stand out in the competitive environment of the logistics market. A strong brand identity not only distinguishes a courier company from its rivals but also helps to leave a lasting impact on clients and consumers. It consists of different aspects that together portray the essence, values, and personality of the company.

Defining the brand's purpose, objectives, and values is crucial to building a distinctive brand identity. This includes defining the purpose of the courier company's existence, its broad aims, and the values that govern its operations. A courier company may connect with its target audience emotionally and express what distinguishes it from competitors by developing a clear and engaging brand mission. Having a distinct brand identity entails generating a distinctive visual identity that represents the business's personality and values. This includes creating a distinctive logo, adopting a consistent color palette, and picking typefaces and pictures that speak to the target demographic.

A well-designed visual identity not only makes the courier company clearly identifiable, but it also communicates professionalism, dependability, and integrity.

Developing a distinct brand identity includes telling a compelling brand narrative that connects with clients and customers. This entails telling the story of the courier company, emphasizing its unique selling characteristics, and demonstrating the value it provides to clients and consumers. A courier company may establish a loyal client base and differentiate itself in the competition by crafting a captivating narrative that elicits emotions and resonates with the target audience.

In addition to a compelling brand narrative, developing a distinct brand identity entails establishing the company's tone of voice and communication style. This involves identifying the language, messaging, and tone that best reflect the brand's identity and appeal to its intended audience.

Maintaining a consistent tone of voice throughout all communication platforms, whether professional and formal or casual and pleasant, helps to strengthen the brand's identity and develop credibility with clients and consumers. A distinct brand identity requires providing a consistent brand experience across all touchpoints. This involves ensuring that all marketing materials, packaging, and digital platforms use consistent branding components like logos, colors, typefaces, and photography. Consistency in the brand experience not only improves brand awareness, but it also fosters confidence and credibility among clients and consumers.

Also, developing a distinct brand identity entails adhering to the company's values and ideals throughout all facets of the organization. This involves providing excellent service, maintaining high levels of professionalism, and continually surpassing client expectations. A courier company may establish a solid reputation and maintain long-term connections with clients and consumers by upholding its brand promise and values.

Identifying target customers and marketing channels.

Identifying target consumers and choosing the appropriate marketing channels are essential stages in starting a successful courier service. This process entails identifying potential consumers' requirements, interests, and habits, as well as selecting the most successful methods for reaching and engaging them.

To begin, a courier firm needs to perform extensive market research to determine its target clients. This entails evaluating demographics, psychographics, and purchasing habits to develop customer profiles that reflect the ideal target population for the company. Understanding the qualities and interests of their target clients enables courier firms to adjust their marketing efforts in order to better contact and connect with them. Selecting target clients necessitates a thorough grasp of their individual wants and pain points regarding courier services.

Businesses in the e-commerce sector, for example, may demand quick and dependable shipping solutions in order to satisfy their consumers' expectations of prompt delivery. Individuals may emphasize price and convenience when selecting a courier service for personal packages. Understanding these specific demands and pain points enables courier firms to properly promote their services, satisfy them, and attract their target clients.

After identifying the target clients, the next step is to choose the best marketing channels to contact them. This entails assessing several marketing channels, both online and offline, to identify which are most suited to reach the target demographic.

For many courier firms, internet marketing platforms provide a low-cost and efficient approach to contacting their target clients. This may include search engine optimization (SEO) to increase the visibility of the company's website in search engine results, social media marketing to interact with potential customers on platforms such as Facebook, Instagram, and LinkedIn, and email marketing to nurture leads and encourage repeat business.

Internet advertising channels such as pay-per-click (PPC) and display advertising can be helpful in reaching out to certain parts of the target audience with tailored messages. Courier firms may use these digital marketing tools to efficiently boost brand recognition, create leads, and drive sales.

In addition to digital marketing channels, offline marketing channels may help you reach your target demographic. This may include traditional advertising methods like print, direct mail, and outdoor advertising, as well as networking events, industry conferences, and trade exhibits. These offline marketing strategies are particularly effective for targeting local businesses and consumers who value human encounters and physical marketing materials.

Defining target consumers and marketing channels entails testing and refining marketing tactics to discover which are most effective at reaching and engaging the intended audience. This may entail A/B testing alternative messaging, graphics, and offers across many marketing platforms to see which connects most with the target demographic.

Finding target consumers and determining the best marketing channels are critical elements in starting a successful courier service. Courier firms can attract clients, boost sales, and achieve long-term success in the competitive logistics industry by understanding their target audience's requirements and preferences and implementing the most effective marketing methods to reach them.

Implementing digital marketing methods.

In today's digital age, a courier service must implement digital marketing methods in order to build an online presence, reach a larger audience, and attract new clients. A courier firm may use digital marketing to efficiently promote its services, create leads, and drive sales by tailoring a number of strategies and approaches to its unique requirements and objectives.

Search engine optimization (SEO) is an important digital marketing approach for courier businesses. SEO is the process of improving a company's website and online content to increase exposure and ranking in search engine results pages (SERPs). A courier firm may enhance organic traffic and attract new clients who are actively looking for shipping and delivery services online by including relevant keywords, providing high-quality content, optimizing meta tags and descriptions, and developing quality backlinks. Employing content marketing methods may help a courier company communicate with its target audience and deliver useful information that meets their wants and worries. This might involve generating blog entries, articles, manuals, and films that provide information on shipping best practices, packing advice, delivery alternatives, and industry trends. By continuously providing excellent and helpful material, a courier company may position itself as a trusted industry leader and attract new consumers looking for relevant information. Email marketing is an effective digital marketing strategy that may help a courier company nurture leads, create client connections, and promote repeat business.

A courier company can send customized email campaigns to subscribers by collecting email addresses via website sign-up forms, online transactions, or lead generation activities. Email marketing enables a courier company to stay top of mind with its clients, boost repeat purchases, and increase engagement with its services.

Employing social media marketing strategies may help a courier company interact with its target audience, raise brand recognition, and generate website traffic. Social media networks such as Facebook, Twitter, LinkedIn, and Instagram allow courier businesses to produce compelling content, communicate with consumers, display their services, and execute targeted advertising campaigns. A courier company may use social media marketing to communicate with new clients, establish a devoted following, and drive conversions.

In addition to these strategies, pay-per-click (PPC) advertising may help a courier service enhance its internet presence and attract new clients swiftly. PPC advertising is the practice of placing ads on search engines and social media platforms and charging a fee for each click.

By targeting relevant keywords and demographics, a courier company may reach potential consumers who are actively looking for shipping and delivery services or viewing relevant internet material.

Executing digital marketing strategies necessitates ongoing monitoring, research, and adjustment to assure efficacy and maximum return on investment (ROI). This entails measuring key performance measures, including website traffic, conversion rates, click-through rates, and cost-per-acquisition (CPA), and using that information to refine and enhance marketing campaigns over time. A courier firm may improve its digital marketing efforts and meet its business goals by examining performance data on a regular basis and making data-driven decisions.

Using standard advertising approaches

Despite the rise of digital marketing channels, conventional advertising approaches continue to be an effective strategy for promoting a courier firm. Traditional advertising approaches include a number of offline tactics for effectively reaching and engaging target audiences in local communities and beyond. While digital marketing has a broad reach and targeting capabilities, conventional advertising tactics provide distinct chances to interact with potential consumers in physical ways and develop a memorable brand presence.

Print advertising is one of the most prevalent conventional advertising tactics, with ads appearing in newspapers, magazines, and local periodicals. Print advertising enables courier firms to successfully reach out to certain geographic regions and target consumers. Print advertising may attract potential clients' attention and build brand recognition by creating eye-catching ads that showcase the courier company's unique services and benefits.

Using outdoor advertising strategies such as billboards, posters, and signs can help boost exposure and reach a larger audience. Billboards placed strategically along major roads or in high-traffic locations may help courier firms grab the attention of both vehicles and pedestrians. Similarly, posters and signs placed in important sites such as shopping malls, transit hubs, and business districts can serve as continuous reminders of the courier company's presence in the area.

Direct mail advertising remains a viable alternative for courier companies seeking to target certain demographics and families with tailored marketing materials. Direct mail campaigns might contain postcards, flyers, brochures, and catalogs highlighting the courier company's services, promotions, and special offers. Courier firms can successfully engage potential clients and generate leads in their local area by creating captivating direct mail pieces and distributing them to targeted mailing lists.

However, participating in local events, sponsorships, and community outreach initiatives may be successful traditional advertising tactics for courier companies looking to enhance exposure and brand familiarity in their regions. Courier firms may engage with potential customers in meaningful ways and demonstrate their commitment to the community by sponsoring local events, attending community fairs and festivals, and supporting charitable initiatives.

Aside from these approaches, conventional advertising includes networking events, industry conferences, and trade exhibitions where courier companies may demonstrate their services, engage with new clients, and build crucial business ties. Courier firms may grow their professional network, generate leads, and remain up-to-date on industry trends and advancements by attending relevant industry events and networking opportunities.

While digital marketing channels have enormous reach and targeting possibilities, conventional advertising approaches are also useful for courier services to engage with potential clients in concrete ways and develop a memorable brand presence. Courier firms may successfully contact their target audience, boost brand recognition, and promote company growth in their local communities and beyond by leveraging print advertising, outdoor advertising, direct mail campaigns, community outreach initiatives, and networking events.

Managing Finance and Budgeting

Managing finances and planning are critical components of running a profitable courier service. Proper financial management ensures that the company runs smoothly, is profitable, and can support long-term development. It entails meticulous planning, monitoring, and allocating financial resources to satisfy the company's operating requirements, cover expenditures, and invest in growth prospects.

Financial management begins with the creation of a detailed budget outlining the courier business's projected income and costs. This entails predicting income from courier services, as well as any other sources such as freight forwarding, expedited delivery, and logistics solutions. On the expenditure side, the budget should include car maintenance, gasoline, insurance, driver and staff salaries, marketing charges, office rent, utilities, and administrative costs.

Once the budget is in place, it is critical to regularly monitor and measure actual financial performance against the budgeted values. This includes regularly evaluating financial statements, such as income statements, balance sheets, and cash flow statements, to analyze the company's financial health and find any anomalies or opportunities for improvement. Regularly monitoring financial performance allows business leaders to make educated decisions, spot possible problems early on, and take remedial steps to guarantee financial stability and profitability.

Good financial management entails establishing ways to maximize cash flow and efficiently manage working capital. This involves keeping enough financial reserves to meet operating expenditures, guaranteeing prompt invoicing and payment collections from customers, negotiating attractive payment terms with suppliers, and successfully controlling inventory levels to minimize excess or outdated stock. By managing cash flow and working capital management, courier firms can increase liquidity, reduce the risk of financial shortages, and support continued operations and growth.

An effective financial management necessitates cautious investment and capital allocation decisions. This includes assessing possible investment possibilities, such as buying new cars, upgrading technology and equipment, increasing service offerings, or entering new markets. Business owners must evaluate the possible rewards and risks involved with each investment before making educated decisions that are consistent with the company's long-term goals and financial capabilities. Money management entails implementing cost-cutting methods and strategies to increase profitability and efficiency. This could include negotiating better deals with suppliers, optimizing routes and scheduling to reduce fuel and labor costs, implementing technology solutions to streamline operations and reduce administrative overhead, and constantly looking for ways to improve operational efficiency and reduce waste.

By efficiently implementing cost-cutting initiatives, courier firms may increase their bottom line and preserve a competitive advantage in the industry.

Successful financial management entails adhering to tax requirements and meeting financial obligations on time. This includes keeping accurate records of income and spending, filing tax returns on time, and paying taxes in accordance with the applicable rules and regulations. Furthermore, company owners must remain current on any changes in tax laws and regulations that may influence their operations and obtain expert guidance as needed to guarantee compliance and reduce tax payments.

Managing finances and planning are critical components of running a successful courier service. Courier businesses can maintain financial stability, improve profitability, and support long-term growth and success in the competitive logistics industry by developing a comprehensive budget, monitoring financial performance, optimizing cash flow and working capital, making prudent investment decisions, implementing cost-cutting measures, and adhering to tax regulations.

Component of managing funds and budgeting for a courier business

1. **Creating a Comprehensive Budget:** A thorough budget is the basis of good financial management. Beyond predicting revenues and costs, other elements to consider include seasonality, market trends, and anticipated demand swings. If business owners may make better judgments and deploy resources if they precisely predict their income and costs.

2. **Monitoring Financial Performance:** Regularly reviewing financial statements and key performance indicators (KPIs) is critical for assessing a company's financial health. This includes evaluating profitability, liquidity, solvency, and efficiency ratios to identify strengths and weaknesses. By spotting patterns and budget irregularities and acting quickly to remedy them, business leaders can preserve financial stability.

3. **Optimizing Cash Flow and Working Capital:** Efficient cash flow management is critical for meeting short-term financial obligations and maintaining day-to-day operations. This includes effectively managing receivables and payables, negotiating favorable terms with suppliers and customers, and ensuring adequate cash reserves. Businesses that optimize working capital can reduce the risk of cash shortages while maintaining financial flexibility.

4. **Prudent Investment and Capital Allocation:** When evaluating investment opportunities, it is critical to conduct comprehensive cost-benefit analyses and assess potential risks. Business owners should prioritize investments that support the company's strategic goals and provide a good return on investment (ROI). Businesses that allocate capital wisely can maximize returns and drive long-term growth.

5. **Implementing Cost-Saving Measures:** Continuously looking for ways to reduce costs and improve efficiency is critical for increasing profitability. This could include renegotiating supplier contracts, optimizing resource utilization, using technology to automate processes, and eliminating unnecessary costs. Businesses that implement cost-cutting measures can gain a competitive advantage and improve their financial performance.

6. **Compliance with Tax Regulations:** Staying compliant with tax laws and regulations is essential for avoiding penalties and maintaining the business's reputation. This includes keeping accurate financial records, filing tax returns accurately and on time, and staying informed about changes in tax legislation. Seeking professional guidance from tax advisors can help ensure compliance and minimize tax liabilities.

7. **Risk Management and Contingency Planning:** Identifying and mitigating financial risks is critical for safeguarding the business against unforeseen events. This may involve diversifying revenue streams, securing insurance coverage for potential liabilities, and developing contingency plans for emergencies.

8. **Long-Term Financial Planning:** Developing a long-term financial plan is essential for achieving sustainable growth and achieving strategic objectives. This involves setting realistic financial goals, establishing milestones for measuring progress, and adjusting strategies as needed to adapt to changing market conditions.

Effective financial management and budgeting require careful planning, diligent monitoring, and proactive decision-making. By creating a comprehensive budget, monitoring financial performance, optimizing cash flow, making prudent investment decisions, implementing cost-saving measures, ensuring compliance with tax regulations, managing risks, and developing long-term financial plans, businesses can maintain financial stability, drive growth, and achieve their strategic objectives in the competitive marketplace.

Estimating startup costs and initial investment

Estimating startup costs and initial investment is a critical aspect of launching a courier business. It requires careful consideration of various factors to ensure adequate funding for essential resources and operations. Startup costs encompass a wide range of expenses, from purchasing vehicles and equipment to covering initial marketing expenses and administrative costs. By thoroughly estimating startup costs and initial investment, aspiring entrepreneurs can create a realistic budget and secure the necessary funding to launch their courier business successfully.

When estimating startup costs, one of the primary considerations is vehicle acquisition. Depending on the size and scope of the courier business, entrepreneurs may need to invest in vans, trucks, or motorcycles to facilitate deliveries. The cost of vehicles will vary based on factors such as size, condition (new or used), and specific requirements for transporting goods safely and efficiently. Entrepreneurs should budget for vehicle maintenance, insurance, fuel, and licensing fees to cover ongoing operational expenses.

In addition to vehicles, entrepreneurs must consider the cost of acquiring the necessary equipment and technology to support courier operations. This may include GPS tracking systems, handheld devices for drivers to manage deliveries, barcode scanners for tracking packages, and software for route optimization and logistics management. Investing in the right technology can streamline operations, enhance efficiency, and improve customer service, but it's essential to budget for these expenses upfront.

Furthermore, entrepreneurs should allocate funds for initial marketing and branding efforts to establish a presence in the market and attract customers. This may include designing a logo and brand identity, creating marketing materials such as business cards and brochures, developing a website, and investing in advertising and promotional activities to generate awareness and attract potential clients. By allocating resources to marketing and branding initiatives, entrepreneurs can effectively position their courier business and differentiate themselves from competitors.

Entrepreneurs must account for administrative costs associated with launching and operating a business. This includes legal fees for business registration and obtaining necessary permits and licenses, as well as accounting and bookkeeping services to manage finances and comply with regulatory requirements. Additionally, entrepreneurs should budget for office space, utilities, office supplies, and other overhead expenses to support day-to-day operations.

Entrepreneurs should consider contingency funds to account for unexpected expenses or challenges that may arise during the startup phase. Having a financial buffer can provide peace of mind and ensure the business remains resilient in the face of unforeseen circumstances.

Creating a financial plan and budget

Creating a financial plan and budget is a crucial step in starting and managing a successful courier business. A well-thought-out financial plan guides the business in achieving its financial goals and details the allocation of financial resources to support operations and growth. By developing a comprehensive financial plan and budget, entrepreneurs can effectively manage their finances, make informed decisions, and navigate the challenges of running a courier business.

To begin creating a financial plan, entrepreneurs must first define their business objectives and establish clear financial goals. This involves identifying short-term and long-term objectives, such as revenue targets, profitability goals, and expansion plans. By setting specific, measurable, achievable, relevant, and time-bound (SMART) goals, entrepreneurs can focus their financial planning efforts and track progress effectively.

Entrepreneurs can proceed to develop a detailed budget outlining the projected income and expenses for the courier business once they establish the business objectives. The budget should include all anticipated revenue streams, such as courier services, freight forwarding, express deliveries, and logistics solutions. Additionally, it should account for various operational expenses, including vehicle maintenance, fuel, insurance, wages for drivers and staff, marketing expenses, office rent, utilities, and administrative costs.

Entrepreneurs should carefully assess their capital needs and prioritize investments that will contribute to the business's growth and long-term success. By allocating resources strategically, entrepreneurs can optimize their budget and maximize the return on investment (ROI) for capital expenditures.

Creating a financial plan involves conducting a thorough analysis of the business's financial health and identifying potential risks and challenges. This includes assessing the business's cash flow, profitability, liquidity, solvency, and efficiency ratios to gauge its overall financial performance. Entrepreneurs can identify areas for improvement, develop strategies to mitigate risks, and improve financial stability by analyzing key financial metrics.

A financial plan necessitates that entrepreneurs establish a regular system for monitoring and tracking financial performance. This involves setting up accounting and bookkeeping processes to record income and expenses accurately, as well as implementing financial reporting systems to generate timely and reliable financial statements. Additionally, creating a financial plan involves developing contingency plans to address potential risks and uncertainties that may impact the business's financial health. This includes building a financial buffer to cover unexpected expenses, such as emergencies, economic downturns, or changes in market conditions.

Creating a financial plan and budget is essential for managing a successful courier business. By setting clear financial goals, developing a comprehensive budget, analyzing financial performance, monitoring progress, and planning for contingencies, entrepreneurs can effectively manage their finances and position their business for long-term success and growth in the competitive logistics industry.

Managing cash flow and expenses

Managing cash flow and expenses is a critical aspect of running a successful courier business. Cash flow management involves ensuring that the business has enough cash on hand to cover its day-to-day operational expenses while also planning for future investments and growth opportunities. By effectively managing cash flow and expenses, entrepreneurs can maintain financial stability, support ongoing operations, and position their business for long-term success in the competitive courier industry.

One of the most important components of managing cash flow. This entails tracking payments from customers for courier services rendered, as well as ensuring timely invoicing and collection of accounts receivable. By implementing efficient invoicing and payment collection processes, entrepreneurs can improve cash flow and ensure that the business has sufficient funds to meet its financial obligations.

Moreover, managing expenses effectively is essential for controlling costs and optimizing cash flow. This includes identifying and categorizing various expenses, such as vehicle maintenance, fuel, insurance, wages for drivers and staff, marketing expenses, office rent, utilities, and administrative costs. Entrepreneurs can improve profitability and ensure efficient resource allocation by closely monitoring expenses and identifying areas for cost reduction or optimization.

Additionally, managing cash flow requires forecasting and planning for future expenses and revenue streams. This entails creating cash flow projections and budgets to estimate incoming cash flows and outgoing expenses over a specific period of time, such as a month, quarter, or year. By forecasting cash flow, entrepreneurs can anticipate potential cash shortages or surpluses and take proactive measures to manage liquidity effectively.

Managing cash flow entails prioritizing payments to vendors and suppliers in order to maintain good relationships and ensure timely delivery of goods and services. To improve negotiating favorable payment terms with suppliers, such as extended payment periods or discounts for early payments, to improve cash flow and maintain positive vendor relationships. By strategically managing vendor payments, entrepreneurs can optimize cash flow and strengthen supplier relationships.

Moreover, managing cash flow and expenses requires implementing strategies to improve working capital management. This includes effectively managing inventory levels to minimize carrying costs and avoid excess or obsolete stock, as well as optimizing accounts payable and receivable processes to improve cash flow. By implementing working capital management strategies, entrepreneurs can improve liquidity, reduce the risk of cash shortages, and support ongoing operations.

Managing cash flow entails establishing contingency plans and reserves to address unexpected expenses or disruptions to cash flow. This includes building a financial buffer to cover emergencies, economic downturns, or unforeseen events that may impact the business's financial stability. By planning for contingencies and maintaining adequate reserves, entrepreneurs can mitigate financial risks and ensure resilience in the face of challenges.

Pricing strategies and revenue generation

Setting effective pricing strategies and generating revenue are crucial components of running a successful courier business. Pricing strategies determine how much customers will pay for courier services, while revenue generation involves maximizing income through various sources. By implementing strategic pricing and revenue generation techniques, entrepreneurs can optimize profitability, attract customers, and ensure the financial health of their courier business.

To begin with, pricing strategies involve careful consideration of various factors, including market demand, competition, operating costs, and customer value perception. Entrepreneurs must assess the value proposition of their courier services and determine the optimal pricing structure to attract customers while ensuring profitability. This may involve offering competitive pricing compared to competitors or implementing value-based pricing based on the unique benefits and features of the courier services provided.

Pricing strategies should take into account the cost structure of the courier business, including vehicle maintenance, fuel, insurance, wages for drivers and staff, marketing expenses, office rent, utilities, and administrative costs. By accurately calculating costs and incorporating them into pricing decisions, entrepreneurs can ensure that prices cover expenses while generating sufficient profit margins. Generating revenue entails diversifying income streams and maximizing revenue from a variety of sources beyond basic courier services. This may include offering additional services such as freight forwarding, express deliveries, logistics solutions, warehousing, and distribution services. By expanding service offerings and catering to diverse customer needs, entrepreneurs can increase revenue streams and enhance the overall profitability of their courier business.

Additionally, revenue generation strategies may involve implementing value-added services or premium service tiers to differentiate the business and command higher prices. This may include offering special delivery options such as same-day or express delivery, package tracking services, signature confirmation, or personalized customer support. By providing added value to customers, entrepreneurs can justify higher prices and increase revenue per transaction.

Revenue generation may involve implementing dynamic pricing strategies based on demand fluctuations, seasonal trends, and other market dynamics. This may include offering discounts or promotions during off-peak periods to stimulate demand, adjusting prices based on supply and demand dynamics, or implementing surge pricing during peak periods of demand. By dynamically adjusting prices, entrepreneurs can optimize revenue generation and maximize profitability.

Effective pricing strategies and revenue generation are essential for running a successful courier business. By implementing strategic pricing decisions, diversifying revenue streams, offering value-added services, establishing strategic partnerships, and implementing dynamic pricing strategies, entrepreneurs can optimize profitability, attract customers, and ensure the financial health and sustainability of their courier business in the competitive logistics industry.

Scaling and Growing Your Business

Scaling and growing a courier business is an exciting yet challenging endeavor that requires careful planning, strategic decision-making, and effective execution. As entrepreneurs seek to expand their operations and capture a larger market share, they must navigate various complexities and considerations to ensure sustainable growth and success in the competitive logistics industry.

The key strategies for scaling and growing a courier business is expanding service offerings to meet the evolving needs of customers. This may involve diversifying service lines beyond traditional courier services to include additional solutions such as freight forwarding, express deliveries, logistics consulting, warehousing, and distribution services. By offering a comprehensive suite of services, entrepreneurs can attract a broader range of customers and capture additional revenue opportunities.

Also, scaling a courier business requires investing in infrastructure and technology to support increased operational capacity and efficiency. This may include upgrading vehicle fleets, implementing advanced routing and logistics software, deploying tracking and monitoring systems, and investing in warehouse facilities. It involves expanding geographic reach and market penetration to reach new customer segments and territories. This may include entering new markets, expanding service coverage to additional cities or regions, and establishing strategic partnerships with local businesses or logistics providers. Expanding their geographic reach, entrepreneurs can tap into new customer bases, increase market share, and drive revenue growth.

In other to develop a scalable courier business, it requires a robust workforce strategy to support increased operational capacity and service demand. This may involve hiring additional drivers, warehouse staff, customer service representatives, and managerial personnel to manage expanded operations effectively. Investing in recruitment, training, and retention programs, entrepreneurs can build a skilled and motivated workforce capable of delivering high-quality service and supporting business growth.

Moreover, scaling a courier business involves implementing effective marketing and branding strategies to increase brand visibility and attract new customers. This may include investing in targeted advertising campaigns, participating in industry events and trade shows, leveraging digital marketing channels such as social media and search engine optimization (SEO), and nurturing existing customer relationships to generate referrals and repeat business. Building a strong brand presence and executing targeted marketing initiatives, entrepreneurs can drive customer acquisition and revenue growth. Additionally, scaling a courier business requires establishing scalable and efficient operational processes and workflows to accommodate increased service demand and transaction volumes.

This may involve optimizing route planning and scheduling, streamlining order processing and fulfillment, implementing automation and technology solutions to improve efficiency, and continuously monitoring and optimizing operational performance. It involves fostering a culture of innovation and continuous improvement to adapt to changing market dynamics and customer preferences. This may include encouraging employee feedback and ideas for process improvement, staying abreast of industry trends and emerging technologies, and actively seeking opportunities for innovation and differentiation in service offerings.

Scaling and growing a courier business requires a multifaceted approach that encompasses expanding service offerings, investing in infrastructure and technology, expanding geographic reach, developing a skilled workforce, executing effective marketing and branding strategies, optimizing operational processes, and fostering a culture of innovation. By strategically planning and executing growth initiatives, entrepreneurs can position their courier business for long-term success and achieve sustainable growth in the competitive marketplace.

Evaluating growth opportunities and expansion strategies

Expanding a courier business necessitates a careful assessment of growth opportunities and the development of effective expansion strategies. Entrepreneurs must assess various factors, including market dynamics, customer needs, the competitive landscape, and internal capabilities, to identify viable growth opportunities and formulate strategies that align with the business's goals and resources.

One key aspect of evaluating growth opportunities is conducting market research to understand industry trends, customer preferences, and emerging opportunities. This involves analyzing market size, growth projections, and demand drivers within the courier and logistics industry. By identifying market gaps, underserved segments, and emerging trends, entrepreneurs can pinpoint growth opportunities and tailor their expansion strategies to capitalize on them effectively.

Growth opportunities necessitates assessing the competitive landscape in order to understand the strengths and weaknesses of existing competitors and identify potential areas of differentiation. This involves analyzing competitors' service offerings, pricing strategies, customer satisfaction levels, and market positioning. By conducting competitive analysis, entrepreneurs can identify opportunities to differentiate their courier business and develop value propositions that resonate with target customers.

Additionally, evaluating growth opportunities involves assessing the business's internal capabilities, resources, and operational readiness to support expansion initiatives. This includes evaluating factors such as financial strength, infrastructure, technology capabilities, workforce expertise, and the scalability of existing operational processes. By assessing internal capabilities, entrepreneurs can identify potential constraints and develop strategies to address them effectively in order to support growth.

Weighing the growth opportunities requires assessing various expansion strategies and determining the most suitable approach based on the business's goals and resources. This may include organic growth strategies such as expanding service offerings, entering new markets, and increasing market penetration, or inorganic growth strategies such as mergers, acquisitions, and strategic partnerships. Evaluating growth opportunities involves developing a comprehensive expansion plan that outlines specific objectives, timelines, resource requirements, and performance metrics for each growth initiative.

This includes identifying key milestones, allocating resources effectively, and establishing accountability mechanisms to ensure the successful execution of expansion strategies. By developing a clear and actionable expansion plan, entrepreneurs can navigate the complexities of growth and minimize the risks associated with expansion initiatives.

Introducing technology for scalability

In today's digital age, using scalability technology is critical to a courier business's development and profitability. Technology helps to improve operational efficiency, provide better customer service, and facilitate corporate development. Entrepreneurs may use the proper digital solutions to improve procedures, maximize resources, and position their courier service for scalability and long-term success.

Route optimization and logistics management are two critical areas where technology can promote scalability in the courier industry. Advanced route optimization software enables organizations to efficiently design and optimize delivery routes, reducing travel time, fuel consumption, and operating expenses. Courier companies may use route optimization technologies to improve delivery efficiency, handle larger order quantities, and scale their operations to meet rising demand without incurring major additional expenditures.

Adopting real-time delivery tracking and monitoring technologies is critical for scalability in the courier sector. GPS monitoring systems and mobile applications allow businesses to follow the whereabouts of cars and shipments in real time, giving consumer's insight into the progress of their delivery. Real-time tracking technology promotes transparency, increases customer happiness, and allows businesses to properly handle higher volumes of deliveries as they grow their operations.

Implementing customer relationship management (CRM) technology is also crucial for scalability in a courier service. CRM software allows organizations to store customer information, track interactions, and analyze consumer behavior in order to customize communications and enhance customer service. Courier organizations can strengthen client interactions, increase customer retention, and scale their operations by integrating CRM technology, all while effectively managing a growing customer base.

Using technology for automated order processing and fulfillment is critical for courier scalability. Automated order processing systems expedite the order intake process, automate order routing, and provide for smooth communication across divisions within an organization. Courier organizations that automate order processing and fulfillment may manage larger order volumes, enhance operational efficiency, and grow their operations without raising administrative costs.

In addition, deploying technology for inventory management and warehouse operations is critical for scalability in the courier industry. Inventory management software helps organizations track inventory levels, manage supply replenishment, and optimize warehouse space. By integrating inventory management systems, courier companies may enhance inventory accuracy, eliminate stock-outs, and scale their operations while effectively managing inventory as they grow.

Additionally, incorporating technology for staff management and scheduling is critical for scalability in a courier service. Workforce management software allows companies to easily arrange shifts, allocate assignments, and track staff performance in real time. By integrating labor management systems, courier organizations may maximize staff usage, increase efficiency, and scale their operations while successfully managing a growing workforce.

Deploying technology for data analytics and business intelligence is crucial for scalability in the courier industry. Data analytics software helps firms examine operational data, discover patterns, and make data-driven choices in order to improve performance and drive development. Using data analytics technologies, courier organizations may obtain important insights into their operations, discover areas for improvement, and grow their operations by making data-driven choices.

Deploying scalability technology is critical to a courier business's development and profitability. Using technology solutions for route optimization, real-time tracking, customer relationship management, order processing and fulfillment, inventory management, workforce management, and data analytics, courier businesses can streamline operations, improve efficiency, and scale their operations to effectively meet rising demand. Entrepreneurs that embrace scalability technology may position their courier service for long-term success and a competitive advantage in the evolving logistics sector.

Expanding services and entering new markets.

Diversifying services and entering new markets are critical strategies for a courier company's growth and expansion. Courier firms that vary their services may cater to a greater range of consumer demands and generate other revenue streams. Similarly, entering new markets helps organizations reach out to new client categories and geographical locations, improving their market share and income potential.

One of the strategies for diversifying services is to go beyond typical courier services and provide consumers with extra value-added services. This might include freight forwarding, expedited delivery, logistics consulting, warehousing, and distribution solutions. By extending their services, courier companies may better address the unique demands of consumers from numerous industries and sectors, boosting their market attractiveness and competitiveness.

Diversification services may entail offering specialized or specialty services tailored to specific consumer segments or sectors. Courier firms, for example, may provide customized services for industries such as healthcare, pharmaceuticals, e-commerce, or perishable commodities, responding to their specific needs and problems. Courier companies may separate themselves from competition and attract consumers looking for customized solutions by providing specialized services.

Entering new markets is also a smart technique for diversifying and increasing a courier business. This may include expanding service coverage to new geographic areas, entering new cities or states, or even expanding overseas. By entering new areas, courier firms may have access to new consumer groups and unexplored revenue prospects, resulting in increased growth and a larger customer base.

It necessitates extensive market research and analysis to understand the target market's demand dynamics, competitive landscape, regulatory environment, and consumer preferences. By conducting extensive market research, courier companies may discover potential growth opportunities and develop targeted plans to effectively enter and capture market share in new areas. Entering new markets may initial strategic collaborations or alliances with local firms or logistical providers to simplify market entry and expansion. In utilizing existing networks and relationships, courier companies may gain access to local experience, infrastructure, and resources, thereby expediting market entry and improving their competitive position in new regions.

Expanding services and entering new markets shows the important of investments in infrastructure, technology, and human resources to support increased operations. This might entail investing in more trucks, equipment, warehousing facilities, and technological solutions to satisfy the demands of new services and markets. As courier organizations diversify and increase their products, they can ensure seamless service delivery and operational efficiency by investing wisely in infrastructure and resources.

For courier businesses, expanding services and entering new areas are critical development and expansion tactics. Courier companies can improve their market share, revenue potential, and competitiveness in the changing logistics industry by providing a wider range of services tailored to client demands and expanding into new geographic regions or customer groups. Courier firms may effectively expand their services and enter new markets with careful planning, smart alliances, and infrastructure and resource investment, resulting in long-term development and profitability.

Creating a long-term, lucrative courier business

Building a viable and lucrative courier business needs a comprehensive strategy that includes operations, customer service, financial management, and expansion initiatives. To stay ahead in a competitive market, it is necessary to establish a firm foundation, prioritize customer happiness, optimize operational efficiency, manage money properly, and innovate constantly.

Creating a sustainable and successful courier business requires defining a defined vision, goal, and set of core values that govern the company's operations and decision-making. This gives the team a sense of purpose and direction, aligns them around similar goals, and aids in the development of a strong business culture focused on providing outstanding service and value to consumers.

Customer satisfaction is critical to creating a long-term and profitable courier service. This includes providing consumers with dependable, responsive, and high-quality service while keeping open communication channels and responding to any issues or concerns as soon as possible. By concentrating on client needs and surpassing their expectations, the courier industry may develop long-term connections, encourage customer loyalty, and generate favorable word-of-mouth recommendations.

In the courier industry, operational efficiency is critical to optimizing profitability. This includes optimizing route planning and scheduling, using technology for real-time delivery tracking and monitoring, expediting order processing and fulfillment, and constantly refining operational procedures to reduce costs and increase efficiency. The courier industry may improve efficiency, lower costs, and increase profits by investing in technology, automation, and process optimization.

Effective financial management is vital for establishing a long-term and profitable courier service. This entails properly assessing initial costs, developing a comprehensive financial strategy and budget, managing cash flow and spending, and tracking important financial KPIs to make informed decisions.

The courier industry can ensure long-term profitability and stability by practicing financial discipline, managing risks, and preparing for long-term sustainability.

In addition to concentrating on core operations and financial management, developing a sustainable and successful courier service necessitates a proactive development and expansion strategy. Diversifying services, entering new markets, forming strategic alliances, and investigating novel business models are all part of capturing new income sources and driving corporate development. By regularly reviewing market prospects, remaining nimble, and adjusting to changing consumer wants and market trends, the courier industry may develop and survive in a dynamic business climate.

A sustainable and lucrative courier business entails investing in talent development, cultivating an innovative and continuous improvement culture, and adopting sustainability methods to reduce environmental impact and positively influence the community.

Conclusion

Finally, beginning a courier service involves careful preparation, smart thought, and a commitment to success. Throughout this comprehensive guide, we've looked at everything from understanding industry dynamics and market opportunities to creating a solid business plan, navigating legal and regulatory issues, and implementing effective operational strategies.

One of the most important lessons from this guide is the value of rigorous market research and feasibility analysis in discovering possibilities and determining the profitability of a courier company endeavor. Aspiring entrepreneurs may make educated judgments and establish a company model that is well-suited to market demands by having a thorough awareness of market trends, client wants, and competition dynamics.

We underlined the need for developing a complete business plan that includes specific objectives, target markets, operational procedures, and financial predictions. A well-thought-out business plan acts as a road map for the company, directing decision-making, recruiting investors or finance, and establishing a framework for monitoring growth and success.

We have also looked at many operational aspects, such as building operational processes, purchasing essential equipment and cars, employing and training employees, managing funds, and using technology for efficiency and scalability. These operational components are crucial to the seamless operation of a courier firm and play a significant part in providing great service to consumers.

In addition, we looked into development and expansion methods such as broadening services, entering new markets, and forming partnerships and networks. These growth initiatives are critical for generating new income streams, extending the client base, and positioning the courier company for long-term success in a competitive industry.

Starting and sustaining a courier service is a complicated enterprise that needs strategic planning, operational excellence, client focus, and the capacity to respond to changing market conditions. By adhering to the concepts mentioned in this guide and constantly innovating and changing, ambitious entrepreneurs may establish a long-term and lucrative courier service that provides value to consumers, promotes growth and prosperity, and has a good influence on the logistics sector.

Final thoughts and inspiration for prospective courier business operators.

For all prospective courier service owners, embarking on this entrepreneurial adventure is both exhilarating and daunting. As you enter the dynamic world of logistics and transportation, keep in mind that success in the courier industry is possible with hard work, endurance, and smart planning.

Most importantly, believe in yourself and your goal. Starting a courier business requires faith in your skills and a strong belief in the value your services can provide to clients. Maintain focus on your goals, and don't be afraid to take measured chances and learn from both wins and disappointments along the way.

Second, never underestimate the value of meticulous investigation and planning. Before you start your firm, spend time learning about market trends, consumer demands, and competitor dynamics. Create a detailed business plan that includes your goals, strategy, and financial estimates. A well-thought-out strategy will act as a road map for your company's growth and expansion, guiding you through each stage.

Prioritize client pleasure above anything else. In the courier industry, dependability, punctuality, and great service are essential. Strive to surpass consumer expectations with each engagement and solicit feedback to further enhance and develop your offerings.

Furthermore, embrace innovation and technology as important success drivers in today's courier sector. Utilize digital solutions for route optimization, real-time tracking, and operational efficiency. Keep up with industry trends and breakthroughs, and be willing to explore new tools and techniques that can improve your business operations and client experience.

Develop excellent ties with your staff, partners, and consumers. Surround yourself with committed and enthusiastic people who share your vision and beliefs. Create a culture of cooperation, communication, and constant learning inside your firm, and create long-term relationships with suppliers, vendors, and clients.

Finally, be adaptive and resilient in the face of obstacles and failures. The courier industry is dynamic and ever-changing; therefore, be ready to pivot, innovate, and adapt to shifting market conditions. Stay devoted to your goals, endure in the face of adversity, and never lose sight of the passion and drive that drove you to start your courier business in the first place.

Finally, keep in mind that starting a successful courier service is a journey that will present both chances and problems. Stay focused, dedicated, and believe in your capacity to overcome challenges and realize your entrepreneurial goals. With dedication, hard work, and a commitment to quality, you can create a long-term and lucrative courier service that improves the lives of your clients while also contributing to the growth and prosperity of your community.

Best wishes on your entrepreneurial venture!

www.ingramcontent.com/pod-product-compliance
Lightning Source LLC
Chambersburg PA
CBHW071054240526
45471CB00015B/1904